Table of Contents

Beach Blanket Set, ***page 2***

Dress Set, ***page 6***

Snow Baby Set, ***page 9***

Christening Set, ***page 14***

Sugar Baby Set, ***page 17***

Beach Blanket Set

Designs by Frances Hughes

Skill Level

Sizes

Fits 8- (10-) inch doll Instructions are given for smaller doll with instructions for larger doll in parentheses. When only 1 number is given, it applies to both sizes.

Finished Measurement

Blanket: 8 x 7½ (9½ x 9) inches

Materials

- SMC Catania (sport weight yarn; 100% cotton; 137 yds/50g per ball): 1 ball each azure blue #0174 (A) and mandarin #0209 (B)

- Size 4 (3.5mm) needles or size needed to obtain gauge
- Embroidery needle
- 3 snaps
- Small amount black felt
- Small amount green and orange embroidery floss
- Fabric glue

Gauge

11 sts and 15 rows = 2 inches/5cm in St st.

To save time, take time to check gauge.

Special Abbreviation

Increase (inc): Inc by knitting on knit rows or purling on purl rows in front and then in back of next st.

Special Technique

Twisted Cord: Tie ends of length of yarn together using overhand knot and attach to doorknob or hook. Insert pencil in loop end and turn like a propeller until entire length of cord begins to kink. Once twisted, continue to hold the twisted end while folding the yarn in the middle. Remove end from doorknob or hook and match ends, then release them allowing the cord to twist on itself. Trim the cord ends and knot each end several times so end won't slip through eyelet.

Blanket

Border

With A, cast on 44 (54) sts.

Knit 2 rows.

Row 1 (RS): Knit across.

Row 2: K3, purl to last 3 sts, k3.

Rows 3–6: Rep [Rows 1 and 2] twice. Cut A.

Rows 7–12: With B, rep [Rows 1 and 2] 3 times. Cut B.

Rows 13–18: With A, rep [Rows 1 and 2] 3 times. Cut A.

Rep [Rows 7–18] 2 (3) times.

Rep Rows 7–12.

With A, rep [Rows 1 and 2] twice.

Purl 2 rows.

Bind off.

Beach Bag

With A, cast on 15 (19) sts.

Knit 4 rows. Cut A.

Row 1 (RS): With B, knit across.

Row 2 (eyelet row): P1, *yo, p2tog; rep from * across.

Row 3: Knit across.

Row 4: Purl across.

Rows 5–26 (32): Rep Rows 3 and 4.

Row 27 (33): Rep Row 3.

Row 28 (34): Rep Row 2. Cut B.

Row 29 (35): With A, knit across.

Knit 4 rows.

Bind off.

Finishing

Sew side seams.

Using A, make 2 twisted cords, each 14 (18) inches long. Weave cords in opposite directions through eyelet row. Tie ends in overhand knot.

Hat

With A, cast on 90 (120) sts.

Knit 1 row. Cut A.

Beg with knit row and B, work 8 (12) rows in St st.

Next row: *K2tog; rep from * across—45 (60) sts.

Next row: Purl across. Cut B.

Band

With A, knit 4 rows. Cut A.

Beg with knit row and B, work 10 (14) rows in St st.

Crown

Row 1: *K2tog; rep from * to last 3 (0) sts, k3 (0)—24 (30) sts.

Row 2 and all even rows: Purl across.

Row 3: [K3, k2tog] 4 (6) times, k4 (4)—20 (24) sts.

Row 5: [K2, k2tog] 5 (6) times—15 (18) sts.

Row 7: *K1, k2tog; rep from * across—10 (12) sts.

Row 9: *K2tog; rep from * across—5 (6) sts.

Cut yarn, leaving 12-inch end. Weave end through sts, draw up to close and sew side seam.

Make a twisted cord 8 (10) inches long and form a bow, sew bow to center back of hat at seam.

Bikini Bottom

Back

With A, cast on 22 (26) sts.

Rows 1 & 2 (RS): Knit across.

Row 3: Purl across.

Row 4: K1, ssk, knit to last 3 sts, k2tog, k1—20 (24) sts.

Row 5: P1, p2tog, purl to last 3 sts, p2tog-tbl, p1—18 (22) sts.

Rep [Rows 4 and 5] 3 (4) times—6 sts.

Crotch

Beg with knit row, work 8 rows in St st.

Front

Row 1: Inc, knit to last 2 sts, inc, k1—8 (10) sts.

Row 2: Inc, purl to last 2 st, inc, p1—10 (12) sts.

Rep [Rows 1 and 2] 3 (4) times—22 (26) sts.

Knit 2 rows.

Bind off.

Sew snaps at waistband on each side.

Referring to photo on page 5, work 5 French knots in orange embroidery floss for flower center, work leaves in lazy daisy stitch using green embroidery floss as desired on each side of French knot.

Bikini Top

For 8-inch doll

With A, cast on 3 sts.

Rows 1–20: Knit across.

Row 21: K1, inc, k1—4 sts.

Row 22: Knit across.

Row 23: K1, [inc] twice, k1—6 sts.

Rows 24–26: Knit across.

Row 27: [K2tog] 3 times—3 sts.

Row 28: Knit across.

Row 29: Inc in each st across—6 sts.

Rows 30–32: Knit across.

Row 33: K1, [k2tog] twice, k1—4 sts.

Row 34: Knit across.

Row 35: K1, k2tog, k1—3 sts.

Rows 36–55: Knit across.

Bind off.

For 10-inch doll

With A, cast on 4 sts.

Rows 1–24: Knit across.

Row 25: K1, inc, k2, inc, k1—6 sts.

Rows 26–31: Knit across.

Row 32: [K2tog] 3 times—3 sts.

Rows 33–35: Knit across.

Row 36: Inc in each st across—6 sts.

Rows 37–39: Knit across.

Row 40: K1, (k2tog) twice, k1—4 sts.

Rows 41–60: Knit across.

Bind off.

Finishing

Work French knots and leaves as for bikini bottom at center front of bikini top.

Sew snap at center back.

Flip-Flops

Sole

For 8-inch doll

With 2 strands of A, cast on 3 sts.

Row 1: K1, inc in next st, k1—4 sts.

Row 2: K1, inc in next st, k2—5 sts.

Rows 3 and 4: Knit across.

Row 5: K1, k2tog, k2—4 sts.

Rows 6–8: Knit across.

Row 9: K1, k2tog, k1—3 sts.

Rows 10–12: Knit across.

Row 13: Sl 1, k2tog, psso. Finish off.

For 10-inch doll

With 2 strands of A, cast on 4 sts.

Row 1: K1, [inc] twice, k1—6 sts.

Rows 2–8: Knit across.

Rows 9 and 10: K1, [k2tog] twice, knit 1—4 sts.

Row 11: Knit across.

Row 12: K1, k2tog, k1—3 sts.

Row 13: Sl 1, k2tog, psso. Finish off.

Upper strap

Cut 4 strands of B, each 10 (12) inches long, tie knot in center of these four strands, tie to sole of flip-flop with 2 strands on each side in toe area and 2 strands on each side in heel area ⅓ inch apart.

Cut felt piece to fit sole and glue to bottom to hide knots.

Rep for other flip-flop. •

Dress Set

Designs by Sue Childress

Skill Level

 EASY

Sizes

Fits 8- (10-) inch doll Instructions are given for smaller doll with instructions for larger doll in parentheses. When only 1 number is given, it applies to both sizes.

Finished Measurement

Blanket: 10½ x 14 (13 x 15) inches

Materials

- SMC Catania (sport weight yarn; 100% cotton; 137 yds/50g per ball): 2 balls white #0106 (A) and 1 ball orchid #0222 (B)

- Size 4 (3.5mm) needles or size needed to obtain gauge
- Stitch markers
- 2 rose appliqués
- ⅓ (½) yard ⅛-inch-wide satin ribbon
- 4- (6-) inch length ¼-inch-wide hook-and-loop tape
- Sewing needle and matching thread
- Fabric glue (optional)

Gauge

11 sts and 15 rows = 2 inches/5cm in St st.

To save time, take time to check gauge.

Special Abbreviation

Increase (inc): Inc by knitting in front and then in back of next st.

Pattern Stitch

Diamond Rib (multiple of 9 sts + 2)
Row 1 (RS): P2, *k2tog, [k1, yo] twice, k1, sl 1, k1, psso, p2; rep from * across.
Rows 2, 4 and 6: K2, *p7, k2; rep from * across.
Row 3: P2, *k2tog, yo, k3, yo, sl 1, k1, psso, p2; rep from * across.
Row 5: P2, *k1, yo, sl 1, k1, psso, k1, k2tog, yo, k1, p2; rep from * across.
Row 7: P2, *k2, yo, sl 1, k2tog, psso, yo, k2, p2; rep from * across.
Row 8: K2, *P7, k2; rep from * across.
Rep Rows 1–8 for pat.

Bonnet

Body

With A, cast on 38 (47) sts.

Knit 1 row.

Work [Rows 1–8 of Diamond Rib pat] 2 (3) times.

Crown

Row 1: *K2tog; rep from * to last 0 (1) st, k0 (1)—19 (24) sts.

Row 2: P1 (0), *p2tog; rep from * to end—10 (12) sts.

Row 3: Knit across.

Row 4: [P2tog] 5 (6) times—5 (6) sts.

Row 5: K1 (0), [k2tog] 2 (3) times—3 sts.

Row 6: Pick up and knit 3 (5) sts along left side, turn; [p2tog] 3 (4) times; pick up and purl 3 (4) sts on other side, turn; [k2tog] 3 (4) times—3 (4) sts.

Row 7: P3 (4) tog. Finish off.

Cut ribbon in half and tie a piece of ribbon at each front edge.

Attach rose appliqué to 1 side of bonnet.

Dress

Beg at neck edge, with B, cast on 38 (47) sts.

Knit 3 (5) rows.

Rows 1–8: Work Rows 1–8 of Diamond Rib pat.

Row 9: K6 (7), bind off 4 (5), k18 (23) including st on needle after bind-off, bind off 4 (5), k6 (7) including st on needle after bind-off.

Row 10: K6 (7), cast on 4 (5), k18 (23), cast on 4 (5), k6 (7).

Row 11: Knit across.

Row 12: Knit across, inc 9 (18) sts evenly across—47 (65) sts.

Rows 13 and 14: Knit across.

Rows 15–17: Rep Rows 12–14—56 (83) sts.

Row 18: Knit across.

Rep [Rows 1–8 of Diamond Rib pat] 2 (3) times.

Bind off.

Attach hook-and-loop tape to back for closure.

Blanket

With A, cast on 64 (73) sts.

Knit 4 rows, placing marker after first 4 sts and before last 4 sts.

Keeping first and last 4 sts in garter st, work [Rows 1–8 of Diamond Rib pat] 11 (13) times on sts between markers.

Knit 4 rows.

Bind off.

Attach rose appliqué to 1 corner of blanket.

Booties

With A, cast on 20 (26) sts.

Knit 6 (8) rows.

Row 1: K5 (8), [k2tog] 5 times, k5 (8)—15 (21) sts.

Row 2: K3 (4), [p3tog] 3 (4) times; k3 (5)—9 (13) sts.

Rows 3 and 4: Knit across.

Row 5: *[K1, p1, k1] all in next st; rep from * across—27 (39) sts.

Row 6: Knit across.

Bind off.

Sew back and bottom seam. •

Snow Baby Set

Designs by Frances Hughes

Skill Level

EASY

Sizes

Fits 8- (10-) inch doll Instructions are given for smaller doll with instructions for larger doll in parentheses. When only 1 number is given, it applies to both sizes.

Materials

- SMC Catania (sport weight yarn; 100% cotton; 137 yds/50g per ball): 1 ball each white #0106 (A), turquoise #0146 (B), red #0115 (C), light green #0219 (D) and lavender #0226 (E)
- Size 4 (3.5mm) straight and double-point (set of 4) needles or size needed to obtain gauge
- 5 snaps

Gauge

22 sts and 15 rows = 4 inches/ 10cm in St st.

To save time, take time to check gauge.

Special Abbreviation

Increase (inc): Inc by knitting on knit rows or purling on purl rows in front and then in back of next st.

Shoes

Note: *Boy's shoe is worked with B, and girl's shoe is worked with D.*

Cast on 22 (26) sts.

Row 1 (RS): Knit across.

Row 2: Purl across.

Rows 3–6: Rep [Rows 1 and 2] twice.

For 8-inch doll

Row 7: K6, k2tog, [k3tog] twice, k2tog, k6—16 sts.

Row 8: Purl across.

Bind off.

For 10-inch doll

Row 7: K8, [k2tog] 5 times, k8—21 sts.

Row 8: Purl across.

Row 9: K6, [k2tog] twice, k1, [k2tog] twice, k6—17 sts.

Row 10: Purl across.

Bind off.

Hat

Note: Boy's hat is worked with B and C, and girl's hat is worked with D and E.

Body

With C *or* E, cast on 44 (52) sts.

Rows 1 (RS)–4 (6): *K2, p2; rep from * across. Cut C *or* E.

Rows 5–17 (7–21): With B *or* D, *k2, p2; rep from * across.

Crown

Next row (Dec row): *K2tog, p2tog; rep from * across—22 (26) sts.

Next row: *K1, p1; rep from * across.

Next row: *K2tog; rep from * across—11 (13) sts.

Cut yarn, leaving a 14-inch tail. Weave end through sts, pull up tight to close. Sew seam.

Pompom

With C *or* E, make small pompom and sew to top of hat.

Boy's Trousers

Note: *Wind small amount of C into 2nd ball for 2nd leg.*

Legs

With each ball of C, cast on 22 (26) sts.

Work both legs *at the same time* with separate balls of yarn.

Rows 1 (RS)–3: Knit across.

Row 4: Purl across.

Beg with knit row, work 9 (13) rows in St st.

Next row (joining row): With same ball of yarn, purl across both legs—44 (52) sts.

Beg with knit row, work 12 (16) rows in St st.

Next row: *K2, k2tog; rep from * across—33 (39) sts.

Next row: Knit across.

Bind off.

Finishing

Sew inside leg seam. Sew center back seam to within 1½ inch of waist. Sew snap at waist.

Boy's Sweater

With B, cast on 44 (52) sts.

Rows 1 (RS)–2 (4): *K2, p2; rep from * across. Cut B.

Row 3 (5): With A, knit across.

Row 4 (6): Purl across.

Rows 5–8 (7–12): Rep [Rows 3 and 4] 2 (3) times.

Row 9 (13): K9 (11), bind off 7 (8), k12 (14) including st on needle after bind-off, bind off 7 (8), k9 (11) including st on needle after bind-off—30 (36) sts.

Cut A.

Row 10 (14): With C, p9 (11), cast on 7 (8) sts, p12 (14), cast on 7 (8) sts, p9 (11)—44 (52) sts.

Row 11 (15): Purl across. Cut C.

Row 12 (16): With A, purl across.

Row 13 (17): Knit across.

Row 14 (18): Purl across.

For 10-inch doll

Rows 19 and 20: Rep Rows 17 and 18.

For both dolls

Row 15 (21): *K1, k2tog; rep from * to last 2 (1) st(s), end k2 (1)—30 (35) sts.

Knit 2 rows.

Bind off.

Sleeves

With RS facing and dpn, join A at center of underarm, pick up and knit 16 (18) sts evenly around.

Divide sts on 3 dpns and knit with 4th dpn.

Knit 14 (16) rnds.

Purl 1 rnd.

Bind off.

Rep for other sleeve.

Finishing

Sew from ribbed waistband to within 2 inches of neck edge. Sew snap at neck.

Girl's Dress

With D, cast on 88 (104) sts.

Rows 1 (RS)–4 (6): *K2, p2; rep from * across. Cut D.

Rows 5 and 6 (7 and 8): With E, *K2, p2; rep from * across.

Row 7 (9): *K2tog, p2tog; rep from * across—44 (52) sts.

Cut E.

Row 8 (10): With A, purl across.

Rows 9–16 (11–18): Beg with knit row, work in St st.

Row 17 (19): K9 (11), bind off 8 (9), k10 (12) including st on needle after bind-off, bind off 8 (9), k9 (11) including st on needle after bind-off—28 (34) sts.

Cut A.

Row 18 (20): With E, p9 (11), cast on 8 (9), p10 (12), cast on 8 (9), p9 (11)—44 (52) sts.

Row 19 (21): Purl across. Cut E.

Row 20 (22): With A, purl across.

Rows 21 and 22 (23 and 24): Work in St st.

Row 23 (25): *K1, k2tog; rep from * to last 2 (1) st(s), k2 (1)—30 (35) sts.

Knit 1 row.

Bind off.

Sleeves

With RS facing and dpn, join A at center of underarm, pick up and knit 16 (18) sts evenly around.

Divide sts on 3 dpns and knit with 4th dpn.

Knit 14 rnds.

Purl 1 rnd.

Bind off.

Rep for other sleeve.

Finishing

Sew from ribbed waistband to within 2 inches of neck edge. Sew snap at neck.

Girl's Panties

Back

With E, cast on 22 (26) sts.

Rows 1 (RS)–4: Beg with knit row, work in St st.

Row 5: K1, ssk, knit to last 3 sts, k2tog, k1—20 (24) sts.

Row 6: P1, p2tog, purl to last 3 sts, p2tog-tbl, p1—18 (22) sts.

Rep [Rows 5 and 6] 3 (4) times—6 sts.

Crotch

Beg with knit row, work 8 rows in St st.

Front

Row 1: Inc, knit to last 2 sts, inc, k1.

Row 2: Inc, purl to last 2 sts, inc, p1.

Rep [Rows 1 and 2] 3 (4) times—22 (26) sts on needle.

Work 4 rows in St st.

Bind off.

Sew snap at each side of waist. ●

Christening Set

Designs by Sue Childress

Skill Level

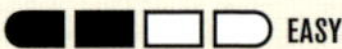
EASY

Sizes

Fits 8- (10-) inch doll Instructions are given for smaller doll with instructions for larger doll in parentheses. When only 1 number is given, it applies to both sizes.

Materials

- SMC Catania (sport weight yarn; 100% cotton; 137 yds/50g per ball): 3 (4) balls white #0106
- Size 4 (3.5mm) needles or size needed to obtain gauge
- Stitch holder
- 2 snaps
- 3 yards (⅛-inch-wide) white satin ribbon
- 8 (9) off-white ribbon roses
- Sewing needle and matching thread

Gauge

10 sts and 12 rows = 2 inches/5cm in shell pat.

To save time, take time to check gauge.

Special Abbreviation

Make 1 (M1): Insert LH needle from front to back under horizontal strand between last st worked and next st on LH needle, k1-tbl.

Pattern Stitch

Little Shell (multiple of 7 sts + 2)
Row 1 (RS): Knit across.
Row 2: Purl across.
Row 3: K2, *yo, p1, p3tog, p1, yo, k2; rep from * across.
Row 4: Purl across.
Rep Rows 1–4 for pat.

Bonnet

Cast on 37 (44) sts.

Knit 2 (3) rows.

Work [Rows 1–4 of Little Shell pat] 6 (8) times.

Crown

Row 1: K1 (0), *k2tog; rep from * across—19 (22) sts.

Row 2: P1 (0), [p2tog] 9 (11) times—10 (11) sts.

Row 3: K0 (1), [k2tog] 5 times—5 (6) sts.

Row 4: P1 (0), [p2tog] 2 (3) times—3 sts.

Row 5: K3tog. Finish off.

Neck edging

With RS facing, pick up and knit 26 (36) sts in ends of rows along neck edge.

Knit 3 rows. Bind off.

Finishing

Cut 18-inch length of ribbon. Weave ribbon through last row of neck edging, leaving long ends for tie. Attach rose on each side of hat at neck edge.

Booties

Cast on 20 (26) sts.

Knit 6 (8) rows.

Row 1: K5 (8), [k2tog] 5 times, k5 (8)—15 (21) sts.

Rows 2–4: Knit across.

Bind off.

Sew back and bottom seam.

Cut 12-inch length of ribbon for each bootie. Beg and ending at center front, weave ribbon through Row 4 and tie in bow.

Referring to photo, attach rose to toe of each bootie.

A christening
is a welcome
to a life in God above—
To all the joy
and blessings
that are part
of His great love.

Panties

Beg at waist, cast on 44 (51) sts.

Knit 4 rows.

Work [Rows 1–4 of Little Shell pat] 3 (4) times.

Next row: K22 (25) sts, turn, placing rem 22 (26) sts on holder for other leg.

Leg

Beg with purl row, work 4 (6) rows in St st.

Next row (Inc row): *P1, M1; rep from * to last st, p1—43 (49) sts.

Next row: Knit across.

Bind off pwise.

Place sts for 2nd leg on needle with RS facing. Join yarn and knit across. Work same as for first leg.

Finishing

Sew inner leg seam. Sew back seam, leaving 1½ inch unstitched below waist. Sew snap at waist. Cut two 12-inch lengths of ribbon. Beg and ending at side seam, weave length of ribbon through Inc row on each leg. Tie in bow and trim ends.

Dress

Beg at yoke, cast on 32 (40) sts.

Knit 2 rows.

Row 1 (RS): K3, [M1, k5] 5 (7) times, M1, k4 (2)—38 (48) sts.

Row 2: Purl across.

Row 3: Knit across.

Row 4: K1 (2), [M1, k5] 7 (9) times, M1, k2 (1)—46 (58) sts.

Row 5: Knit across.

Row 6: Purl across.

Row 7: Knit across.

Rep [Rows 5–7] 1 (2) time(s).

Next row: K9 (11), bind off 5 (8), k18 (20) including st on needle after bind-off, bind off 5 (8), k9 (11) including st on needle after bind-off—36 (42) sts.

Next row: K9 (11), cast on 8 (10) sts, k18 (20), cast on 8 (10) sts, k9 (11)—52 (62) sts.

Next row: K2tog, knit across—51 (61) sts.

Knit 5 (7) rows.

Inc row: K1, *M1, k1; rep from * to last 1 (0) st, k1 (0)—100 (121) sts.

Work [Rows 1–4 of Little Shell pat] 12 (14) times.

Next row: *K1, M1; rep from * to last st, k1.

Next row: Purl across.

Bind off kwise.

Sew back seam to Inc row. Sew snap at back neck edge. Referring to photo, sew roses on front yoke.

Cut 18-inch length of ribbon. Beg and ending at center front, weave through Inc row on yoke. Tie in bow and trim ends.

Sleeves

Cast on 23 (30) sts.

Knit 1 row.

Rep [Rows 1–4 of Little Shell pat] 2 (3) times.

Knit 4 rows.

Bind off.

Finishing

Sew sleeve seams.

Sew cast-on edge of sleeves into sleeve openings. Cut two 10-inch lengths of ribbon. Beg and ending at center of sleeve, weave ribbon through edge. Tie in bow and trim ends. •

Sugar Baby Set

Designs by Frances Hughes

Skill Level

EASY

Sizes

Fits 8- (10-) inch doll Instructions are given for smaller doll with instructions for larger doll in parentheses. When only 1 number is given, it applies to both sizes.

Materials

- SMC Catania (sport weight yarn; 100% cotton; 137 yds/50g per ball): 1 ball each light blue #0173 (A) and light pink #0158 (B)
- Size 4 (3.5mm) needles or size needed to obtain gauge
- 2 snaps

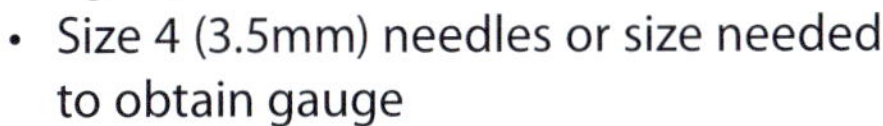

Gauge

11 sts = 2 inches/5cm in St st.

To save time, take time to check gauge.

Pattern Stitch

Lace (multiple of 6 sts + 7)
Row 1 (RS): K1, *yo, p1, p3tog, p1, yo, k1; rep from * across.
Rows 2, 4 and 6: Purl across.
Row 3: K2, yo, sl 1, k2tog, psso, yo, *k3, yo, sl 1, k2tog, psso, yo; rep from * across to last 2 sts, k2.
Row 5: P2tog, p1, yo, k1, yo, p1, *p3tog, p1, yo, k1, yo, p1; rep from * across to last 2 sts, p2tog.
Row 7: K2tog, yo, k3, yo, *sl 1, k2tog, psso, yo, k3, yo; rep from * across to last 2 sts, sl 1, k1, psso.
Row 8: Purl across.
Rep Rows 1–8 for pat.

Bonnet

With A, cast on 74 (98) sts.

Rows 1 and 2: Knit across.

Row 3: Purl across.

Rows 4–9 (11): Beg with knit row, work in St st.

Row 10 (12) (Dec row): *K2tog; rep from * across—37 (49) sts.

Row 11 (13): Purl across.

Rows 12–19 (14–29): Work [Rows 1–8 of Lace pat] 1 (2) time(s).

For 8-inch doll

Rows 20–23: Work Rows 1–4 of Lace pat.

Crown

Row 1: K1, *k2tog, k1; rep from * across—25 (33) sts.

Rows 2 and 4: Purl across.

Row 3: K1 (0), *k2tog, k1; rep from * across—17 (22) sts.

Row 5: K1 (0), *k2tog; rep from * across—9 (11) sts.

Row 6: Purl across. Cut A, leaving a 12-inch tail.

Weave end through rem sts, pull up tight to close and sew seam.

Rose

Make 2

With B, cast on 27 sts.

Rows 1 and 3: Knit across.

Row 2: Purl across.

Row 4: *K3tog; rep from * across. Cut B, leaving a 12-inch tail.

Weave end through rem sts, pull up tight to close. Coil piece to form a rose. Sew 1 rose to hat along brim Dec row below Lace pat.

Sew other rose aside for ruffled top.

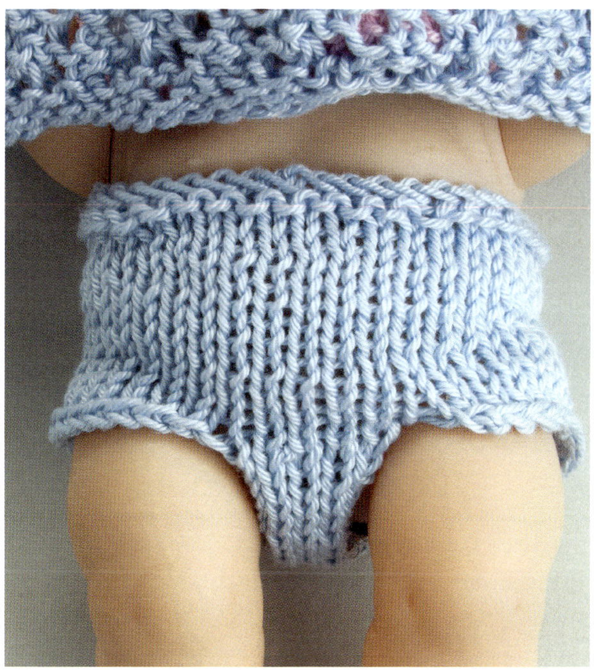

Panties

With A, cast on 42 (50) sts.

Rows 1–3: Knit across.

Row 4: Purl across.

Rows 5–14 (16): Beg with knit row, work in St st.

Row 15 (17): Bind off 18 (21) sts, k6 (8) including st on needle after bind-off, bind off rem 18 (21) sts.

With WS facing, join A; beg with purl row, work 16 rows in St st for crotch. Bind off.

Finishing

Place ends of rows tog to form back seam and sew from lower edge to within 1 inch of waist. Sew crotch to center back where joined.

Sew a snap to upper waistband edge at center back.

Ruffled Top

With B, cast on 85 (97) sts.

Row 1: Purl across. Cut B.

Row 2: With A, purl across.

Rows 3–10: Work Rows 1–8 of Lace pat.

Row 11: K1, *k2tog, k1; rep from * across—57 (65) sts.

Row 12: Purl across.

Row 13: K13 (15), bind off 7 (8), k16 (18), bind off 7 (8), k12 (14)—43 (49) sts. Cut A.

Row 14: With WS facing and B, p13 (15), cast on 7 (8), p17 (19), cast on 7 (8), p13 (15)—57 (65) sts.

Row 15: Purl across. Cut B.

Row 16: With A, purl across.

Rows 17–18 (20): Work in St st.

Row 19 (21): K1, k2tog, k0 (2)—38 (44) sts.

Knit 2 rows. Bind off.

Finishing

Referring to photo for placement, sew set-aside rose to front yoke. Sew snap to back neck edge. •

General Information

Abbreviations & Symbols

[ ] work instructions within brackets as many times as directed
( ) work instructions within parentheses in the place directed
** repeat instructions following the asterisks as directed
* repeat instructions following the single asterisk as directed
" inch(es)

approx approximately
beg begin/begins/beginning
CC contrasting color
ch chain stitch
cm centimeter(s)
cn cable needle
dec decrease/decreases/decreasing
dpn(s) double-point needle(s)
g gram(s)
inc increase/increases/increasing
k knit
k2tog knit 2 stitches together
kwise knitwise
LH left hand
m meter(s)
M1 make one stitch
MC main color
mm millimeter(s)
oz ounce(s)
p purl
pat(s) pattern(s)
p2tog purl 2 stitches together
psso pass slipped stitch over
pwise purlwise
rem remain/remains/remaining
rep repeat(s)
rev St st reverse stockinette stitch
RH right hand
rnd(s) rounds
RS right side
skp slip, knit, pass slipped stitch over—1 stitch decreased
sk2p slip 1, knit 2 together, pass slipped stitch over the knit 2 together—2 stitches decreased
sl slip
sl 1kwise slip 1 knitwise
sl 1pwise slip 1 purlwise
sl st slip stitch(es)
ssk slip, slip, knit these 2 stitches together—a decrease
st(s) stitch(es)
St st stockinette stitch
tbl through back loop(s)
tog together
WS wrong side
wyib with yarn in back
wyif with yarn in front
yd(s) yard(s)
yfwd yarn forward
yo (yo's) yarn over(s)

Standard Yarn Weight System

Categories of yarn, gauge ranges and recommended needle sizes

Yarn Weight Symbol & Category Names	0 LACE	1 SUPER FINE	2 FINE	3 LIGHT	4 MEDIUM	5 BULKY	6 SUPER BULKY
Type of Yarns in Category	Fingering 10-Count Crochet Thread	Sock, Fingering, Baby	Sport, Baby	DK, Light Worsted	Worsted, Afghan, Aran	Chunky, Craft, Rug	Super Chunky, Roving
Knit Gauge Range* in Stockinette Stitch to 4 inches	33–40 sts**	27–32 sts	23–26 sts	21–24 sts	16–20 sts	12–15 sts	6–11 sts
Recommended Needle in Metric Size Range	1.5–2.25mm	2.25–3.25mm	3.25–3.75mm	3.75–4.5mm	4.5–5.5mm	5.5–8mm	8mm and larger
Recommended Needle U.S. Size Range	000 to 1	1 to 3	3 to 5	5 to 7	7 to 9	9 to 11	11 and larger

*** GUIDELINES ONLY:** The above reflect the most commonly used gauges and needle sizes for specific yarn categories.

** Lace weight yarns are usually knitted on larger needles and hooks to create lacy, openwork patterns. Accordingly, a gauge range is difficult to determine. Always follow the gauge stated in your pattern.

Skill Levels

BEGINNER

Beginner projects for first-time knitters using basic stitches. Minimal shaping.

EASY

Easy projects using basic stitches, repetitive stitch patterns, simple color changes and simple shaping and finishing.

INTERMEDIATE

Intermediate projects with a variety of stitches, mid-level shaping and finishing.

EXPERIENCED

Experienced projects using advanced techniques and stitches, detailed shaping and refined finishing.

Inches into Millimeters & Centimeters

All measurements are rounded off slightly.

inches	mm	cm	inches	cm	inches	cm	inches	cm
⅛	3	0.3	5	12.5	21	53.5	38	96.5
¼	6	0.6	5½	14	22	56.0	39	99.0
⅜	10	1.0	6	15.0	23	58.5	40	101.5
½	13	1.3	7	18.0	24	61.0	41	104.0
⅝	15	1.5	8	20.5	25	63.5	42	106.5
¾	20	2.0	9	23.0	26	66.0	43	109.0
⅞	22	2.2	10	25.5	27	68.5	44	112.0
1	25	2.5	11	28.0	28	71.0	45	114.5
1¼	32	3.2	12	30.5	29	73.5	46	117.0
1½	38	3.8	13	33.0	30	76.0	47	119.5
1¾	45	4.5	14	35.5	31	79.0	48	122.0
2	50	5.0	15	38.0	32	81.5	49	124.5
2½	65	6.5	16	40.5	33	84.0	50	127.0
3	75	7.5	17	43.0	34	86.5		
3½	90	9.0	18	46.0	35	89.0		
4	100	10.0	19	48.5	36	91.5		
4½	115	11.5	20	51.0	37	94.0		

Knitting Basics

Cast-On

Leaving an end about an inch long for each stitch to be cast on, make a slip knot on the right needle.

Place the thumb and index finger of your left hand between the yarn ends with the long yarn end over your thumb, and the strand from the skein over your index finger. Close your other fingers over the strands to hold them against your palm. Spread your thumb and index fingers apart and draw the yarn into a "V shape."

Place the needle in front of the strand around your thumb and bring it underneath this strand. Carry the needle over and under the strand on your index finger.

Draw through loop on thumb.

Drop the loop from your thumb and draw up the strand to form a stitch on the needle.

Repeat until you have cast on the number of stitches indicated in the pattern. Remember to count the beginning slip knot as a stitch.

Cable Cast-On

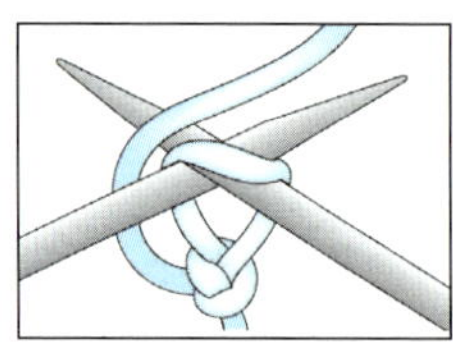

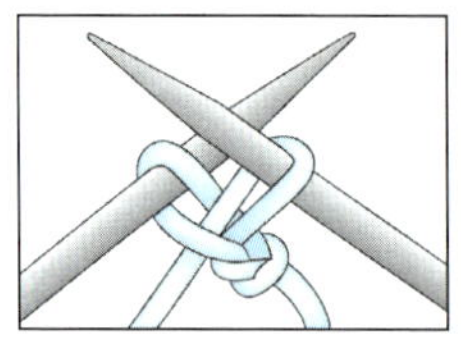

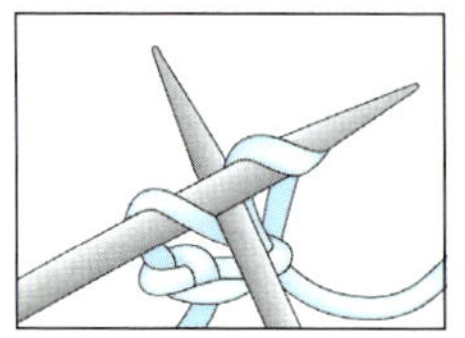

This type of cast-on is used when adding stitches in the middle or at the end of a row.

Make a slip knot on the left needle. Knit a stitch in this knot and place it on the left needle. Insert the right needle between the last two stitches on the left needle. Knit a stitch and place it on the left needle. Repeat for each stitch needed.

Knit (k)

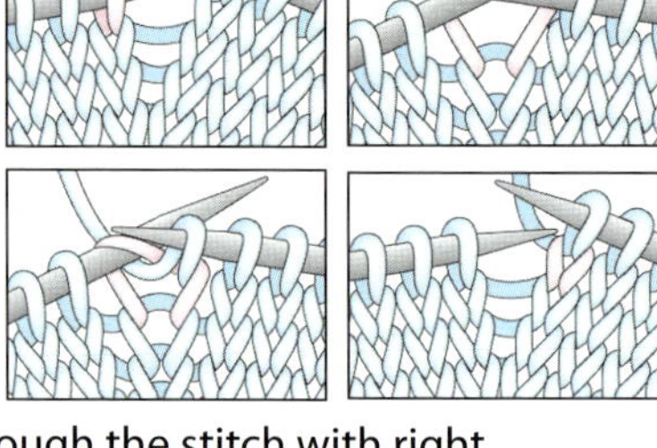

Insert tip of right needle from front to back in next stitch on left needle.

Bring yarn under and over the tip of the right needle.

Pull yarn loop through the stitch with right needle point.

Slide the stitch off the left needle. The new stitch is on the right needle.

Purl (p)

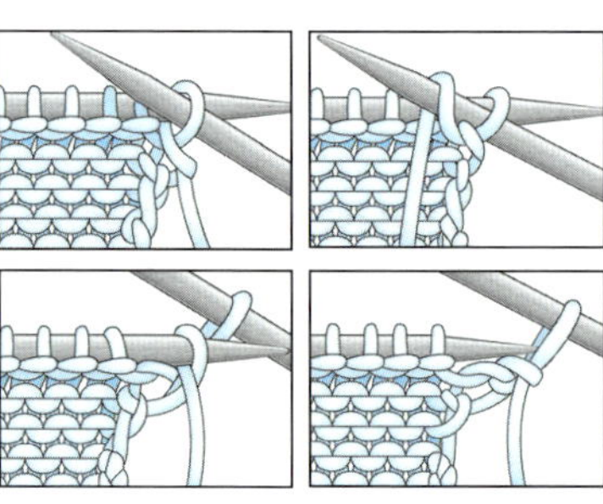

With yarn in front, insert tip of right needle from back to front through next stitch on the left needle.

Bring yarn around the right needle counterclockwise.

With right needle, draw yarn back through the stitch.

Slide the stitch off the left needle. The new stitch is on the right needle.

Bind-Off

Binding off (knit)

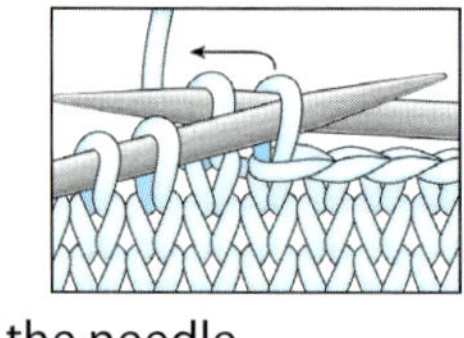

Knit first two stitches on left needle. Insert tip of left needle into first stitch worked on right needle and pull it over the second stitch and completely off the needle.

Knit the next stitch and repeat. When one stitch remains on right needle, cut yarn and draw tail through last stitch to fasten off.

Binding off (purl)

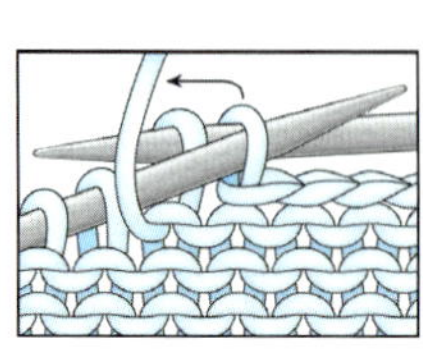

Purl first two stitches on left needle. Insert tip of left needle into first stitch worked on right needle and pull it over the second stitch and completely off the needle.

Purl the next stitch and repeat. When one stitch remains on right needle, cut yarn and draw tail through last stitch to fasten off.

Increase (inc)

Two stitches in one stitch

Knit increase (kfb)

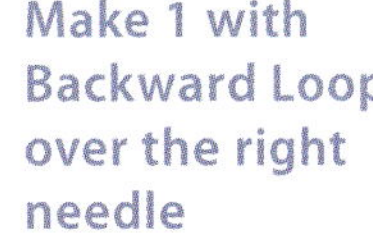

Knit the next stitch in the usual manner, but don't remove the stitch from the left needle. Place right needle behind left needle and knit again into the back of the same stitch. Slip original stitch off left needle.

Purl increase (pfb)

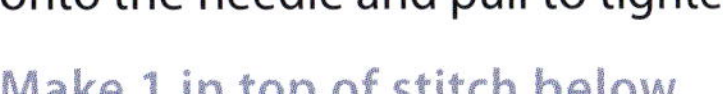

Purl the next stitch in the usual manner, but don't remove the stitch from the left needle. Place right needle behind left needle and purl again into the back of the same stitch. Slip original stitch off left needle.

Invisible Increase (M1)

There are several ways to make or increase one stitch.

Make 1 with Left Twist (M1L)

Insert left needle from front to back under the horizontal loop between the last stitch worked and next stitch on left needle.

With right needle, knit into the back of this loop.

To make this increase on the purl side, insert left needle in same manner and purl into the back of the loop.

Make 1 with Right Twist (M1R)

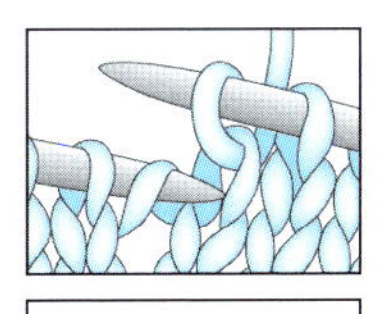

Insert left needle from back to front under the horizontal loop between the last stitch worked and next stitch on left needle.

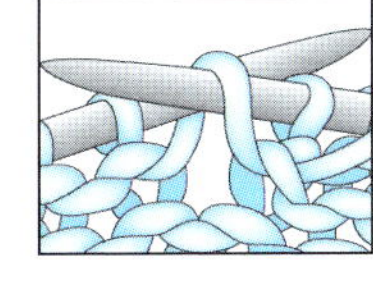

With right needle, knit into the front of this loop.

To make this increase on the purl side, insert left needle in same manner and purl into the front of the loop.

Make 1 with Backward Loop over the right needle

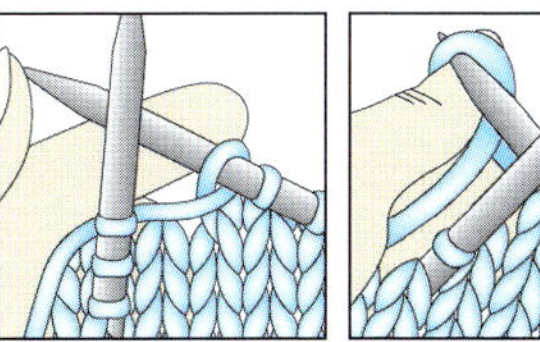

With your thumb, make a loop over the right needle.

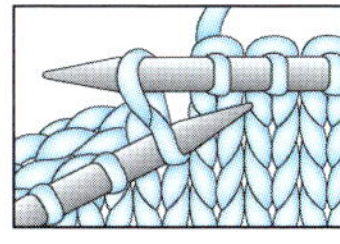

Slip the loop from your thumb onto the needle and pull to tighten.

Make 1 in top of stitch below

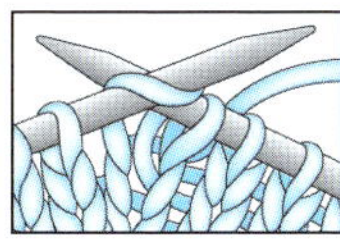

Insert tip of right needle into the stitch on left needle one row below.

Knit this stitch, and then knit the stitch on the left needle.

Decrease (dec)

Knit 2 together (k2tog)

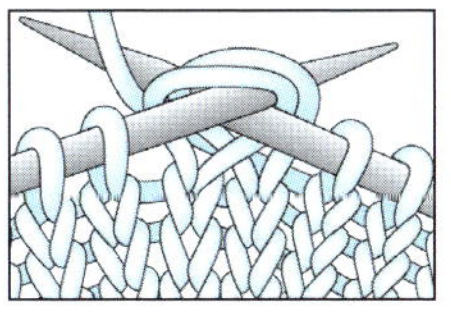

Put tip of right needle through next two stitches on left needle as to knit. Knit these two stitches as one.

Purl 2 together (p2tog)

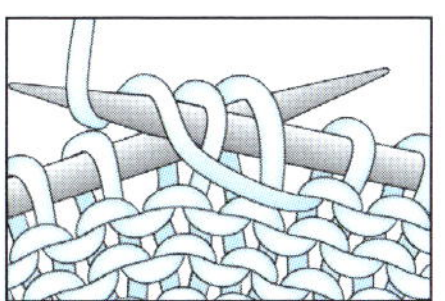

Put tip of right needle through next two stitches on left needle as to purl. Purl these two stitches as one.

Slip, Slip, Knit (ssk)

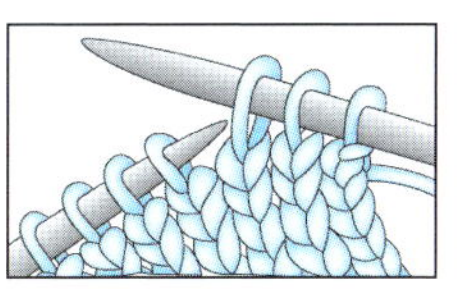

Slip next two stitches, one at a time, as to knit from left needle to right needle.

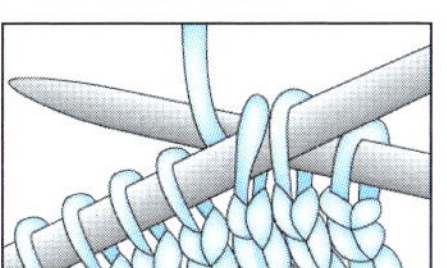

Insert left needle in front of both stitches and knit them together.

Slip, Slip, Purl (ssp)

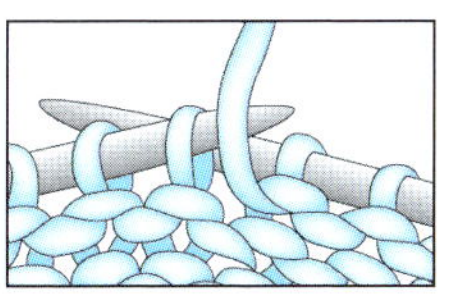

Slip next two stitches, one at a time, as to knit from left needle to right needle. Slip these stitches back onto left needle keeping them twisted.

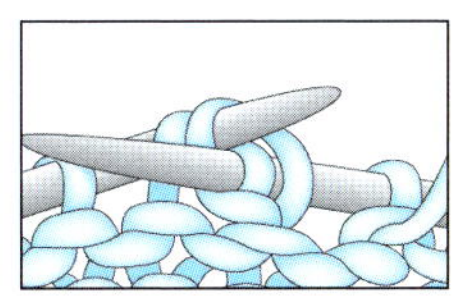

Purl these two stitches together through back loops.

Lots to Love Babies Doll Clothes is published by DRG, 306 East Parr Road, Berne, IN 46711. Printed in USA.

ISBN: 978-1-59217-358-7

1 2 3 4 5 6 7 8 9

Photo Index

2

14

6

9

17